The Buck Stops With You

The Buck Stops With You

When Leaders Lead, Employees Become Motivated

John Graci

iUniverse, Inc.
New York   Bloomington

iUniverse books may be ordered through booksellers or by contacting:

iUniverse
1663 Liberty Drive
Bloomington, IN 47403
www.iuniverse.com
1-800-Authors (1-800-288-4677)

ISBN: 978-1-4401-6659-4 (sc)
ISBN: 978-1-4401-6661-7 (ebook)

Printed in the United States of America

iUniverse rev. date: 12/17/2009

Acknowledgements

Thank you to Ross Reishus, who has been my mentor for the past 10 years. Ross' unique ability to communicate practical, down-to-earth leadership truths and techniques has led to the success of thousands of supervisors and managers.

A special debt of gratitude goes to Susan Esekdahl, Executive Vice President of Employers Association, Inc. who not only encouraged me to undertake this endeavor, but provided the financial support.

Appreciation also goes to all my colleagues at Employers Association whose input and support provided me the opportunity to complete this project.

Finally, my wife, Lori, along with our two kids, Gina and Matthew, thank you for providing me the gift of encouragement.

Contents

Preface

Hostage: A student who <u>doesn't</u> want to attend a training class, seminar or presentation for any number of reasons but has been told to do so. Usually this objection to attending is due to the student's distorted judgment that multiple years of experience as a manager equates to knowing all there is in management.

During a recent presentation, one of these hostages had a profound impact on me, spurring me to write **_The Buck Stops With You_**! I overheard the hostage telling another participant prior to my seminar, that his attendance at **_Motivating Employees Using Common Sense_** was going to be a waste of his precious time because he had 20 years of experience as a manager.

Prior to kicking off my presentation, the human resources professional who hired me, gave me some insight on one unwilling participant. The HR professional said this hostage would likely give me a hard time and that I should not feel the least bit shy about hurting the hostage's feelings or possibly using this hostage to make a point with the rest of the leaders. I thanked the HR professional for the scouting report.

Near the beginning of my presentation, I asked the question, "How many of you <u>don't</u> want to be here today?" I guess you could say it was my way of breaking the ice just a bit not only with this hostage, but any other prisoners lurking in the audience. Predictably, the hostage along with a few others shot their hand straight up. I then said, "If any of you don't want to be here today, who do you have a debate with? If you are thinking me, I just figured out why you are here today! If you do not want to be here, you have a debate with the person who asked you to be here. Make their life miserable if you must, but please be respectful to me and others here today. I'm here to make your jobs as leaders easier."

Feeling a bit blindsided, the hostage raised his hand and said, "What can you do to make my life easier as a manager?" I thanked this person for their valid question. I then asked, "What is currently happening on your team today that is causing you concern?" The hostage replied he had a bunch of employees who were demotivated. I thanked this person for their situation and kindly asked how many people work for you today? The prisoner responded, "About half!" The audience chuckled in amusement. I then asked the prisoner if I could ask him a couple of questions to better understand his situation. Predictably, he agreed.

My first question centered on whether he felt at all responsible for the attitude of his employees. He simply responded, "It is hard to find good people these days!" I asked him why he felt compelled to throw his employees under the bus and wash his hands of any responsibility for their current attitudes. He simply looked at me with a confused and dazed look. I said,

"In my professional opinion, you want to play the victim. You feel as though you are entitled to motivated employees." I then proceeded to explain all the obligations he and everyone else in the audience had to fulfill as a leader. If anyone was unwilling to perform any of these obligations they could not sit here and complain about the attitude of their employees. I wound up our brief conversation by saying, "The next two hours will greatly benefit your team, your career and the folks who brought me here today because ... "

The Bucks Stops With You!

On that day, the hostage inspired me to write a book on how often managers like to blame their employees for having poor attitudes, yet are unwilling to look in the mirror and ask what they could have done to cause their employees to react this way. Managers who feel entitled to motivated employees or who enjoy, *"Passing the buck"* on their leadership responsibilities will greatly benefit from

The Buck Stops With You!

Obligatory Disclaimer:

I have one very important point to make on the tone and content of this book. As a professional speaker and trainer, audiences have recognized me for my tell-it-like-it-is presentation style. Since audiences find my folksy approach refreshing and entertaining, it made sense that I maintain this tone in

The Buck Stops With You!

I do not profess to be an English language authority. In fact, I may even butcher the English language to drive home a learning point. My goal as a communicator of change is not to demonstrate how bright I am, but to relate the power of a leader as best I can, in a manner that is straightforward and easy to understand.

Chapter 1
The Buck Stops With You

Can a leader motivate an employee?

Can an author motivate you?

If you answered yes to either of these questions, I just figured out why you need to read this book. All motivation is self-motivation. <u>You</u> make the choice to work faster, harder and smarter each day at home or at work.

Ever have a good day? Who made the choice to have a good day? Ever have a bad day? Who made the choice to have a bad day? You did of course! You probably don't believe that yet, but you always have a choice. This buck stops with you!

If managers can't actually motivate employees, then what's the big deal about employee motivation? Leaders have an opportunity and an obligation to create a positive work place for their employees. As a leader creates a positive place to work, the employee will make choices to work faster, harder and smarter.

How do leaders create a positive place to work? Here's a clue. It doesn't cost any money and falls under a leader's control. Management consultant and best selling author Tom Peters had it right when he said, "Bosses ought to get off their high horses and quit viewing themselves as motivators. The average employee, 18-58 years old, comes to the workplace fully endowed with motivation. Our primary role as leaders is to clear the silly B.S. out of the way and let the troops get on with the job!"

Management is a profession, and as with any profession it requires study and training. If you don't think management is a profession, go to your local bookstore and take an inventory of how many books there are on being a better leader. The list of titles seems endless. What the majority of these books have in common is they are long on theory and short on practical application. They all tell you what is important when it comes to managing employees, but they fall short in providing specific skills to help improve the efforts of your employees.

You won't find any theories in this book. It contains practical down-to-earth techniques to help create a positive place to work for your employees.

CAUTION: Every technique discussed in this book falls within your authority. You don't need to ask your boss's permission to apply these techniques. If by any chance, you make the choice to not apply your knowledge, you can't go back to the local bar after work and sit and complain about the attitude of your employees. You see, the buck stops with you on the application of these skills.

Take a look at the bell curve, nature's law of distribution. Apply any statistics or data to the bell curve and it is inevitable the data will fall into Unsatisfactory, Marginal, Average, Good or Excellent classifications.

What does the bell curve have to do with a profession? Not every professional, be they an accountant, doctor, dentist, human resource generalist, machinist and yes, a leader can be excellent. According to nature's law of distribution, some professionals fall into the average portion of the bell curve and some fall into the unsatisfactory or needs-improvement portion of the bell curve based on their skills. Every boss you've ever worked for fits into one of these categories.

Which boss did you like working for: the boss whose leadership skills fell into the unsatisfactory/marginal portion of the bell curve, or the boss with skills clearly in the good/excellent portion? Where would you like to see your current boss on the bell curve? Where does your current boss see you on the bell curve? Where do you see yourself on the bell curve? Keep in mind, all self-perception is distorted. Leaders typically have a better perception of themselves than others have of them. Most importantly, where do you think your employees would like to see you on the bell curve?

Since some leaders fall into the unsatisfactory portion, it's a good idea to know why. One of the most common complaints heard from employees is <u>their managers don't listen</u>.

Chapter 2
To Gain Respect, Listen Up

Think of the worst managers you ever worked for. I bet they did a wonderful job of not listening to you. In fairness, most managers do not choose to be a poor listener; they just don't know how to be good.

When leaders choose not to listen to employees, they don't involve their employees, and when they don't involve employees, the employees don't bring any energy to work and everyone's job becomes harder. In fact, I am aware of managers who don't listen to their employees as often as their employees like to be listened to. Those managers often find their names appearing on restroom walls throughout their facility! A quick way to gain respect from your employees is to listen to their ideas and suggestions.

Over the years, I have asked managers and supervisors how they go about listening to their employees. Most often I hear the response, "I ask my employees if anybody has any ideas or questions." I ask those leaders where they learned how to listen to their employees that way. I get some confused and dumbfounded looks, but eventually we determine that they asked "Does anybody have any questions or ideas?" because their teachers or managers taught them that way.

Let me show you how some managers keep opening the door on their own noses when it comes to listening to *anybody* instead of *everybody*. I'll illustrate my point with a typical team meeting.

Prior to your team meeting, your boss comes looking for you. He tells you that a customer order has to be completed by the end of the day. The boss admits he is clueless on how to meet this deadline. He just looks at you and says, "That's why I've got you on the payroll!" The boss's departing bit of advice for you is to ask your employees for their ideas.

What do you do next? Predictably, you get everyone together and ask, "Does anyone have any ideas on how we can meet this deadline?"

Rookie is the first person on your team to raise a hand. Rookie is a little wet behind the ears, or shall we say naïve. Rookie offers an idea to make your job easier.

Mr. Sarcasm, another employee on your team, offers his two cents. Mr. Sarcasm earned his reputation by letting people down real easy. Once Mr. Sarcasm gets wind of Rookie's idea, he replies sarcastically, "Rookie, are you on drugs? That idea will never work!"

Let's think about what just happened. Rookie's reward for throwing out an idea to make your job easier is criticism. Shot down in front of the rest of the group, will Rookie be more likely or less likely to give you an idea again in this or any other meeting? Less likely of course.

There is another employee on your team. His name is Clam. Clam has not given an idea in five years. He just sits there in each meeting doing his best imitation of a bobble head doll. Having just watched Mr. Sarcasm shoot down Rookie's idea, do you think Clam will be motivated to give an idea? How about others on the team? Do you think they will feel comfortable in giving an idea knowing the consequence? I suspect not.

Let's fast forward two days later with this hypothetical situation. Your boss comes downstairs to your office with another request. Your boss reminds you that once a year the organization formally recognizes the efforts of their employees via Employee Appreciation Day. The boss then asks you to come up with some new ideas, so they can be forwarded to the Employee Appreciation Day committee. Once again, the boss's departing words of advice for you are to ask your employees for their ideas and suggestions.

What do you do next? Predictably, you get everyone together and ask, "Does anybody have any ideas?" The first person to throw their hand up in this meeting is not Rookie. He learned his lesson two days ago: shut up or risk being criticized in front of the rest of the group. The first person to raise their hand this time happens to be Mr. Sarcasm.

Mr. Sarcasm has another nickname on the team, "*Party Time*." It is always 4:30 p.m. in the back of this employee's mind. *Party Time* likes to party and this Employee Appreciation Day smells like another party. Once *Party Time* throws out an idea to make the leader's life easier, who is hiding in the weeds? That's right,

Rookie! It is now payback time in Rookie's mind. Rookie fires back, *"Party Time,* that idea is so retro, do you still live in the '80's?" *Party Time's* reward in this meeting is outright criticism, shot down in front of the team.

Remember Clam? It's been five years and two days and he still has not given a good idea. He just sits there. Will he be motivated to offer an idea? Nope! How about everybody else on your team—what are the odds they will they speak up knowing the possible consequence? Slim and none, and slim just left town!

Ever hear the expression, "Every action has as an equal and opposite reaction?" In a short period of time the manager will tell their boss they were only able to come up with one idea for Employee Appreciation Day. In disgust, the boss will reply, "What? Only one idea? You are kidding me, right?" Now, here is where I see plenty of managers passing the buck by blaming their employees.

The typical manager might attempt to save their backside from being chewed out by saying, "Boss, I have been meaning to talk to you about my team. You see, they have a bunch of bad attitudes. I would like to recommend a teambuilding class for my team." Now, do we have a bunch of employees in need of a teamwork class, or do we have a manager who lacks the skill to listen to all of his employees?

Can you see where some managers who lack the skills to lead a group of employees would love to blame their employees at this point? In fairness to the manager, he is doing what other people have taught him to do when it comes to listening to employees. Most managers are very good at listening to anybody, but deficient in listening to everybody. It's not enough to want participation, you need an effective way to get it.

How do you listen to everybody on a team as opposed to anybody? The technique is called Circle Six. Don't get hung up on the number, it works great with groups of two to ten people. If you only have one person on your team it is easy to listen to them. But with greater numbers of people, how do you listen to everybody's ideas, opinions or factual information?

Circle Six

First, choose a topic.

Second, appoint yourself the chairperson/scribe.

Third, allow people time to think. It is only common courtesy to allow people time to think.

Think back to high school, junior high or elementary school. What happened when the teacher called on you and you were not ready to give an answer? That's right, your mouth engaged before your brain had a chance to kick in. How did that make you feel in front of the rest of the class? Like an idiot! Let your employees gather their thoughts for 10 seconds or if you would like, overnight. It is your meeting, you determine the time limit based on the subject.

Fourth, as chairperson, gather one idea at a time from each person. As you gather each idea, there can be no discussion or criticism. The chairperson should just be saying, "Next, no discussion."

9

One important point, if you have a ground rule limiting employees to provide their ideas in 10 seconds, and you have an employee who continues to speak past the time limit, the chairperson should simply respond, "Next, let's move on!"

Is it rude to interrupt a talker during one of your meetings? Nope. I call it being assertive. Nature's law of distribution says you are likely to have a talker on your team. These are people who like to dominate your team meetings. If you have a talker on your team, how long will your meeting last? As long as the talker wants it to last! Let's be ruthlessly honest for a moment; when these talkers (a.k.a. dominators) are talking a mile a minute, what does everybody else want the manager to do? That's right, shut them up!

What happens if an employee doesn't want to give an idea? All they have to say is, "Pass." They don't have to give an answer, but if they choose not to answer they can't complain to other teammates that the manager does not listen. Employees, behind the leader's back will start to support the leader by stating, "Hey, the boss does a wonderful job of listening to us, you just choose not to give any ideas!"

Employees have an expectation that a leader who attempts to listen to them will act on their input or follow up a short time later and let them know why it is not a good idea. Thus, if you do not get back to people regarding the status of their precious ideas, they are less likely to give you information in the future. Managers who make choices not to follow up on their employees' ideas will inevitably groom employees with bad attitudes. Who gave them the bad attitude? The manager did!

I do my best research in bars. Don't get me wrong, I am not promoting bars, but I like to go where my customers like to go after work to see if the material I am teaching is current.

I recall just last year having my favorite beverage at a local bar in the Twin Cities. A group of managers were sitting around a table and discussing work-related issues. I heard one manager chime in, "I do a great job listening to my employees. They never complain." I thought to myself, here is another manager who is busy patting himself on the back about how great a listener he happens to be, yet I suspect the reality is the exact opposite of what it appears.

I would *want* employees to complain on my team. I like complainers. They have no problem coming right into your office and telling you what other employees are saying behind your back! The reality of this situation is that employees possess ideas and suggestions to make the leader's job easier. As a boss, hearing from my manager that the employees never complain would concern me.

Albert Einstein said the definition of insanity is doing the same thing over and over and being stunned nothing ever changes. Some managers cannot figure out why they keep on opening the door on their noses. Some managers are their own worst enemy. Managers need to be more proactive than ever in gaining information from their employees.

The following scenario reflects a manager once again about to open a door on their nose and they don't even see it coming. During a meeting, a manager begins to ask for ideas, input or concerns from their team. An employee with plenty of initiative offers an idea to make the manager's job easier. Then the manager, in front of the rest of the team states, "That is a great idea! Now, you run with that idea!" Watch what happens the next time there is a meeting and the manager asks for ideas. Mr. Initiative will think twice about giving an idea or concern. It is rather obvious what's going on in this employee's mind: you provide an idea and you get more work to do.

Some managers are very good at punishing employees who come up with the ideas, simply because they believe the old expression, "Employees bring more energy to their own ideas." Well it's true, employees *do* bring more energy to their own ideas, however, managers cannot continually punish the employees providing input. In the future, a manager may even question whether this employee, with a history of giving ideas and suddenly not offering input, just might be getting a bad attitude. The key question is: who gave this employee a bad attitude? The manager did by delegating only to the most cooperative and willing employee as opposed to other employees on the team.

The number one complaint employees have of their managers is their managers do not listen. Most of your employees will appreciate their leader doing a Circle Six. In order to lessen resistance, make sure you remind them of the benefits. The Circle Six technique allows you to listen to *everybody* and not just anybody. The leader controls the subject, who is talking and how long everyone talks. Finally, Circle Six reduces the time of a typical meeting.

Chapter 3
No Benefit to a Poor Relationship

The moment anyone gets promoted into a management position there is not one benefit to a poor relationship with any employee or co-worker. When there is friction between a manager and any of their employees, alliances naturally begin to form. Take for instance a poor relationship between a manager and the quietest person on the team. That quiet person will build alliances because they do not like coming to work everyday and being possibly the only person at odds with the manager. Power in numbers is their rule of thumb. Managers who do not strive to improve relationships with all their employees create a negative place for their team to work. The result is an allied bunch of demotivated employees.

Earlier, I said most employees appreciate a leader running a Circle Six. Truthfully, a few employees may not appreciate the leader listening to everyone. On every team or group, there will be people who naturally have influence among the team members. These people have the same job title as everyone else on the team; however they also have influence with the team but they lack the responsibility that goes along with it. These people are known as informal leaders.

Informal leaders can be rookie or veteran. They can be positive or negative. Show me a group of people who get together each week, and I will show you one or two who have influence over everyone else. Informal leaders can be found on all teams. They are not bad people, they just have influence with the rest of the group.

If you wonder who your informal leader is, try this experiment. The next time you communicate some negative news to your employees, look over your shoulder as you walk away and notice whose desk, workstation or piece of machinery people are surrounding. That is your informal leader.

The informal leader is the employee with influence. What's important to keep in mind about an informal leader is they have been leading your team meetings since day one. In the past, if the manager asked the team for ideas, that was the signal for the informal leader to start giving ideas. Informal leaders may actually get their nose bent out joint if you try a Circle Six because you are now attempting to listen to everybody on the team and not just them. Anticipate their reaction and communicate the benefits of the Circle Six technique.

If a leader has a great relationship with the informal leaders, it can make the leader's job much easier. For instance, a leader's got some negative information to communicate to their team, such as mandated overtime on a Friday afternoon. If the leader anticipates the employees will not like this news, the leader can simply pull the informal leader aside before the meeting, and spend a little extra time helping the informal leader understand how the leader or company arrived at this decision. Later, when the leader formally communicates this negative news to the rest of the team, the leader can be assured the informal leader is supporting the leader behind his or her back.

However, if the manager has a poor relationship with the informal leader, when the manager communicates the negative news and leaves the meeting, the manager can be assured the informal leader is stabbing the manager right in the back in front of the rest of the team. Now whose job just got harder?

I spend hours flying around the country. I had a memorable conversation with a passenger a few years ago, that drives home the importance of a leader striving to improve relationships. As we stowed our luggage and settled into our seats, the passenger on my right extended his right hand and said, "Hi, I am Jack." I naturally introduced myself as John. Jack asked what I did for a living. I said, "I teach people to be nice." Jack responded, "Seriously, what do you do for a living?" I looked at this passenger and, trying my best to be coy, said, "I teach people to use their common sense." Jack looked at me a little frustrated and blurted out, "Say, if you do not want to talk during the flight, just say so." I instantly responded, "I am being honest with you about what I do. I am a Leadership Training Consultant. I teach leaders on every level to treat employees the way they want to be treated." Jack then said in an off-handed manner, "You have a very practical job description!" He then began turning his attention to a newspaper.

About 10 minutes later, Jack looked at me and said, "I have been thinking about what you do for a living. If I was your only customer you would starve!" I didn't know what he meant, so I asked him to clarify. He gloated, "I have 20 years of management experience and never attended a management training class."

He went onto say he was a born manager. Feeling a bit professionally disrespected, I responded in a casual attitude, "Jack, do you have an open mind?" Jack replied quickly and confidently, "Well, yes, you have to be open-minded as a vice president." I then reminded Jack the true meaning to having an open mind is a person cannot form a rebuttal until the other person is done talking. I said, "If you never attended a management training class, I suspect you graduated from the school of hard knocks." Jack replied, "I guess you can say that." I quickly followed up by noting, "Oh yes, the school of hard knocks, where everyone graduates as long as you suck up precious oxygen." Jack smiled and turned his head ever so slightly to the right. I could sense he was getting ready to form a rebuttal, so I quickly noted, "Don't forget, you said you had an open mind, you are not going to respond until I am finished talking." Jack readjusted himself in chair and said, "Okay, you're right."

I then asked, "Have you ever heard the expression, 'Self-perception is typically distorted'?" Jack, looking a little defensive and inquisitive, asked, "What do you mean?" I simply said, "Managers often have a higher perception of themselves than what their employees have of them." Fearing I may have caught him off guard, Jack blurted out, "I know what you are trying to do. Those one-liners may work to shake your students' confidence, but they are not going to work on me!" I looked at Jack, and said, "Well, maybe you are a born manager. I just wanted to have fun with you. You seem like you have some thick skin, so I just wanted to see how you would react."

I asked Jack, "As vice president, is there a manager, or executive you don't get along with for one reason or another?" Jack replied sarcastically, "There are a few shmucks out there!" I followed up by asking if he was aware if any of his employees knew of him not getting along with another member of management." Jack replied, "Well of course. My employees are not blind or stupid." I interrupted him quickly, "How do your employees react to the other manager's team knowing you don't get along with their manager?" He did not answer. "I will tell you how they react, Jack. Your team feels as though they have to support you by not getting along with the other team." "What you are getting at?" Jack said impatiently. I added, "Well, I've got to believe that teamwork is something you encourage or strive for everyday with your team. The amount of teamwork you get out of your own team will rise no higher than what you demonstrate with your employees. You are a role model. Monkey see, Monkey do! I guess they never taught you that in the school of hard knocks. One more thing, if you choose not to get along with other managers, sending your team to a teambuilding class will not work, because you gave them permission not to get along." Jack stared at me very quietly, and then said, "I never thought about it that way."

A few minutes later, Jack asked that I provide him another example of what he might be doing wrong. I said, "Hey Jack, I normally charge people for this material, but I will give you one more thing to think about." I then asked him, "Has there ever been a time at work where your boss asked you to communicate some negative news to your team, news you didn't like?" Jack replied, "Welcome to my world!" I asked, "Did your employees sense you did not like this change or negative news?" Jack replied, "Like I said, they are not stupid!" I added, "How much energy do you think your employees will bring to accepting change, when they know you do not even support it yourself?" Jack just shook his head from side to side. I continued, "One more thing to keep in mind, Jack. If you as a manager do not support the change, then you can't complain about your employees' attitude." Jack looked at me and said, "You really know how to hit a guy below the belt."

The moment an employee becomes a manager is the moment they are thrust into the position of role model. A manager cannot give his employees a speech on the importance of working as a team, and then bad mouth other managers a short time later. The amount of teamwork a manager gets out of his or her team will rise no higher than what the manager demonstrates working with other people in the organization.

Prior to being promoted to any leadership position, most employees are concerned about one thing: they are held accountable for getting their work done. Their primary duties are what they are being held accountable for doing. However, once promoted, managers are often judged not only on their ability to get work done through others, but also on the relationships they have with their current team and co-workers including their boss. Managers on every level should ask themselves "How friendly should I get with my employees both on and off the job?" Unlike thirty years ago, very few managers get any guidance or direction regarding this issue today.

Over the years I have interviewed many managers on how friendly they think they should get with their current team. Since many managers lacked any direction, they handle this issue the way a parent or previous manager had once advised them. The rule of thumb I encourage managers to think about is: perception is reality. Don't bother giving your employees a speech on how you do not play favorites. The employees will make their own determination based on what they see with their own eyes.

Let's take a look at a few situations to underscore my point so you can make your decision on how friendly you should get with your employees both on and off the job. Let's say you were to go fishing or shopping over a weekend with some friends of yours who happen to report to you at work. Come Monday, what will you talk about with these people? Yes, the highlights and lowlights of that weekend. What do you suppose those employees who did not attend your fishing or shopping trip will be thinking? They most likely will perceive favoritism. Favoritism smells of double standards in the eyes of human resource professionals.

Is this a problem? Let's say you were to go to a local bar after work with two friends of yours, who again, report to you at work. While talking with your friends, you notice some other teammates across the room chatting. You, as the manager, begin to feel a little uncomfortable about this situation, so you look at your two friends and say, "We are not going to talk about work."

Let's let our common sense kick in just a bit. What happens after a few drinks? Yes, you begin talking about work. As a manager, you really start to feel uncomfortable about this situation, so you make a choice that you will not talk about work at all. You essentially do not participate in the conversation taking place at your table. What might your silence project to your friends sitting at the table? Agreement! They might think to themselves, "Oh, the manager knows what we are talking about; he just can't say anything because he is the manager."

Those non-friends of yours across the way who are on your team, what will they perceive as they glance over at your table? They will perceive you are talking about work, and maybe even them! You are not even participating in your table's conversation, yet it is the perception that you are that will get you every time.

When it comes to delegation, if you delegate a task to a

friend of yours from the team, what will your non-friends think? Favoritism and maybe how your friends always get the developmental projects. If you take that same task and delegate it to non-friend, now what will the non-friends think? Why do we always get the difficult or menial tasks?

I remember attending a management training class at a local college just to see what our competitors were teaching. The topic of transitioning into a leadership position came up during class. The professor said, "If a manager is ever put into a position of authority and they need to delegate, always delegate to the most qualified employee to prevent other employees of thinking of favoritism." I raised my hand and asked the professor, "What if there is a friendship to consider, I mean what if the manager is friends with the most qualified person?" The professor looked at me and said, "What part of most qualified employee did you not understand?" The rest of the class just laughed. I felt a bit embarrassed with all the laughter, so I sat back down. I began thinking I could justify how bright I was regarding this topic and how out of touch the professor sounded regarding this topic, however I just swallowed my pride. I reminded myself that I was there to scout the competition and when you see them going the wrong way, let them go. In fairness, to the professor, he probably never spent a day in the trenches ever having to consider how friendly to get with his employees. It does make a difference because "Perception is reality."

A final situation to reflect on involves performance reviews. The manager needs to judge their employees' performance. If the manager gives a non-friend a negative performance review, what do you suppose the non-friend will chalk that rating up to? Yes, "I got this rating because I am not close to the boss." If the manager gives a friend a negative performance review, what may they chalk that up to? They might be thinking they received this unfavorable rating because the manager has to be tougher on them because of the friendship. If the manager gives this friend a positive performance rating, what may the friend chalk this up to? "The close friendship I have with the manager is paying dividends!" Whichever way it's interpreted, though the manager's assessment might be accurate, it may be perceived differently by the employee.

There is an expectation from employees and upper management that a leader is not going to play favorites. How can you meet that expectation if your actions say otherwise? If you have a friendship, what should you do? I personally, would sit down with this friend and explain the obligation and expectations you have to fulfill as a leader. If your friend looks at you and says, "This job is going to your head," *News Flash—they are not your friend.* If they are your friend, they will understand the pressures and expectations that go along with your new job and let you off the hook.

I never encourage managers to break off personal relationships; however, I do encourage managers to cool their friendships at work. Most employees will appreciate the manager taking measures to distance themselves from their friends when at work. However, if the manager chooses to maintain this relationship outside of work, I can offer no guarantees.

A manager who chooses to get as friendly as they want with employees and could not care less what non-friends may perceive would be guilty of creating a negative place to work for some employees. A non-friend may become demotivated because they assume they have no chance to get promoted as long as the boss is spending more time with certain other employees. A leader needs to balance their time with all of their employees. Don't think it doesn't matter. Don't give your employees speeches how you do not play favorites. Employees will make their own determination based on what they perceive, because perception is reality.

Chapter 4
Not Everyone Is Like You

After years of conducting leadership training classes and public speaking engagements, a familiar comment I hear from attendees is that I possess a firm grasp of the obvious. They often ask how I got that way. I simply respond, "It is my odd value system!" We all have a value system. If you have a belly button, then you have a value system.

According to Dr. Morris Massey, (who is in my opinion the father of values programming) values are events, conditions and experiences that we lived through growing up and even during our adult life. These experiences program or condition us with a way of looking at the world—giving us our point of view. Values help you decide what to buy, how to vote, what to reject or accept. What does a belly button and value system have in common? We had no say in obtaining either. You were born with a belly button and when it came to your value system, a bunch of events and influences were dumped on you conditioning how you look at the world.

When we do not agree with someone else's value system, we often will mutter to ourselves, "you're odd." Your employees might be saying the same about you. From someone else's perspective, based on their experiences, we are all abnormal. The key issue with values is that some managers either intentionally or unintentionally impose their value system on their employees, yet they have the nerve to ask the employees to work faster, harder and smarter. Very demotivating!

Your family plays a role in programming how you look at the world. When I was seven, my father pulled his snowblower out of the garage, and within half an hour, removed eight inches of snow from our driveway. All I did was walk behind my father in my parka and snowmobile boots. As my father began wiping the snow off the snowblower and storing it in the garage, I began to walk toward the front door of the house. My father shouted, "John, where are you going?" I replied, "In the house." My dad quickly replied, "No, you're not. I want you to grab your red shovel." I curiously asked why. My dad said, "We are not done yet clearing the driveway." My dad continued, "I want you to grab your shovel and I am going to get my shovel. The snowblower does not clean the driveway perfectly. It left some snow and tracks on the driveway. When the sun comes out tomorrow, I want the blackest driveway in our neighborhood!"

Day after day, year after year, I skimmed my dad's driveway. Today, if you were to come into our development, guess who has the blackest driveway in our neighborhood! That is the way a driveway should always look in my eyes. I raise my eyebrow when I see my neighbors not showing the same diligence when shoveling their driveway. I sometimes wonder why they do not keep their driveway as clean as mine. Bottom line, they think I am abnormal, I think they are abnormal.

What do my shoveling habits have to do with leading a group of employees? Between my shoveling experiences and few other family experiences, I can be a perfectionist. More importantly, I have an intense need to pay attention to details. I have worked with a few people over the years who didn't share my same passion for perfectionism and detail. I suspect they looked at me as being odd, and I thought they were a bit odd.

For years, during team meetings, I would get criticized by other employees for asking too many questions. If we had a problem, I found it natural to ask: who, what, where, when, why and how. However, there were some "odd" employees and managers who were offended by my problem solving efforts. They were not as disciplined as me about gathering facts but they were very creative. They would rather pull solutions out of some part of their anatomy then take the time to better understand the situation. In fact, I had one boss tell me that I had a bad attitude in meetings because of my need to ask so many questions. After being hammered over the years, I became very reluctant to contribute in meetings because of the consequences that went along with asking questions.

I personally have a high need to be recognized. Once again, my father played a wonderful role in programming me. My father is retired and very handy. He will help me out around the house when he has a chance, or call me at 10 P.M. telling me what he did and how he defied all odds in getting something fixed.

One night, after dad called late in the evening, my wife asked, "Was that your dad?" I nonchalantly said, "Yeah. Boy he felt pretty good about fixing that gazebo door for us." My wife fired back, "Who are you trying to kid? You are just like your father. You like to hear from others how you make a difference." Keep in mind, I am the type of person who, if you can bring facts to my attention as opposed to your opinion, I am more apt to accept your comments. I looked at my wife and said, "Give me an example of my high need of recognition." My wife was obviously ready for my challenge. She reminded me of a game I assembled for my son one Christmas. She reminded me of how I whined when the directions said it would take an amateur 20 hours to assemble, and a handy person 4 hours. Truthfully, I thought for sure it would take me a full 40 hours to assemble. It took me 12 hours. My wife kindly reminded me that I told everyone in the entire family over the remaining holidays how I defied all odds to get it done in only 12 hours!

What does recognition have to do with leading a group of people? Consider employees who like to hear often they make a difference. If they don't hear it often enough, work becomes a negative place for them. They might make choices not to work faster, harder and smarter, and maybe the ultimate choice, not show up for work.

Some managers don't think their job is to communicate with or recognize an employee. Some managers choose not to recognize as often as they are capable of because their manager does not recognize them and they choose to emulate their manager.

Once, I was teaching an onsite leadership class for an agriculture company located in northern Missouri. There were about twenty people in the class. I decided to go with the Circle Six listening technique in order to listen to all the experiences they had recognizing an employee. I gave all the students 30 seconds to summarize a recognition experience they had the previous week. They were to answer the following questions:

- Who did you recognize?

- What did this person do worthy of recognition?
- What reaction did you receive from the recognized person?

All students chose to participate in the Circle Six, except for the very last student. When the student said, "I'll pass. I didn't have time to do my assignment." I simply responded, "That's quite all right. You've got the rest of your life to apply your knowledge." The rest of the class seemed amused by my response.

The student then said, "To be perfectly honest, I made a choice not to recognize anybody this week. Employees are already getting paid to do a good job." I asked the student where they ever heard that employees get paid to do a good job. The student indicated his mom had told him it's already in an employee's paycheck; in addition, he heard the same phrase from past bosses. I asked the student in front of the rest of the class my favorite question, "Do you have an open mind?" The student confidently answered, "Yes." I then asked the rest of the class, how many of them would like to work for this student, knowing in advance he was not going to recognize them, because it was already in their paychecks. Not one of the other students raised their hand! I then looked at the student and said, "Are you taking note of what just happened?"

A short time later, during a break, the student thanked me for creating an awakening in his eyes. Personally, I don't call them awakenings. I refer to them as significant emotional events (S.E.E.). According to Dr. Morris Massey, a S.E.E. is some event or condition which occurs in one's life, jarring up their value system and causing them to throw out a precious value. Values go down deep in people. They do not get rid of them like yesterday's newspaper.

Over the years, I have had attendees tell me they experienced mini-significant emotional events during class, causing them to change. Other significant emotional events include death or illness of a family or friend, marriage, divorce, birth of a child, filing bankruptcy, getting fired, joining the military, or watching planes crash into the World Trade Center and Pentagon. Reading a book or watching a movie can also sometimes create that event.

Values come from a number of different sources. Family, friends, the type of school you attended, level of education, geography, media, gender and culture can all contribute to one's odd value system. Generation-Xers (born 1965-1979) are fast and efficient on computers, but can be a little difficult to manage. This generation has gained a reputation of being "Know-it-alls." Baby Boomers, (born 1946-1964), seem to have trouble working with Generation-Xers because their value systems are different. Gen-Xers have an understanding of today's computer and internet that most Baby Boomers will never attain.

If you're a Baby Boomer, try not to tell Xers how to do things. Instead, tell Xers what you want and let them deliver the results. Allow them to use their own ingenuity and decision making skills. If you do, I suspect your Xers might just work faster, harder and smarter, because their leader trusts them!

Many Xers grew up believing there will not be any Social Security for them when they retire because the Baby Boomers will have beaten them to it. Yes, Xers watch television and they hear how the Social Security system needs to be overhauled because the Baby Boomers are going to implode it before Xers get a chance to get apply for their retirement benefits. The bottom line; Xers have a high need to grow and develop. They like to work for leaders who play a role in their development.

Most Baby Boomers have that same need to grow and develop too. Many of them have seen their parents lose their jobs after working 20 years for a company. Generation-Y (born 1980-2000) a.k.a. Millennials, do not easily trust managers older than them. Generation-Y is not impressed with job titles of Generation-Xers and Baby Boomers. They often witnessed their parents climbing the corporate ladder, enjoying a successful career and income, then—**wham**—get laid off during tough times.

Generation-Y employees were raised by helicopter parents— parents that hovered over their children. When their parents gave their teens cell phones, it created a double-edged sword. The teen experienced new freedoms, however since their parent is only a speed dial away, they often times did not make decisions on their own. These kids grew up with their parents scheduling every minute of their day. When these employees come to work, they may find it perfectly normal to continually ask others how to do their job as opposed to using their best judgment and acting independently.

Generation-Y employees question the judgment of why Baby Boomers and Generation-Xers work 45-60 hours per week. Generation-Y wants to be judged on what they get accomplished and not the number of hours they work.

How would you like to work for a manager who imposed their value system on you day after day at work? I suspect you wouldn't. Managers who impose their value systems on their employees often wonder why these employees make choices not to work faster, harder and smarter. These same managers will often find time to go to the proverbial local bar after work and complain how their employees work styles and attitudes are different than their own. Sounds like insanity.

A manager should not have to give up their value system at home. However, at work that manager needs to find areas of compromise among value systems. If it is always the manager's value system, then coming to work becomes a negative place to be for employees.

Earlier, I touched on the topic, "How friendly should managers get with their employees both on and off the job?" I've had a few students and keynote attendees tell me in private that they will get as friendly as they want with their employees, and the heck with what others on their team may be thinking. That would be an example of a manager imposing their value system on their employees, and then they are stunned when their employees get a bad attitude. As the old expression says, common sense just isn't that common!

Chapter 5
Coaching or Lecturing?

Do employees make mistakes on purpose? According to nature's law of distribution, some do, however I suspect most do not. Confronting an employee when they make a mistake can be an uncomfortable situation for any manager. Few managers look forward to the possibility of hurting an employee's self-confidence or facing friction during the discussion. When an employee makes a mistake, a leader has an obligation to determine if the leader has met their responsibility to train the employee. The next time an employee makes a mistake, here is a coaching technique that will focus on the situation as opposed to the employee.

Ask the employee, "What happened?" When you ask them this question the tone of your voice should be calm. If the employee responds they do not know what happened, a leader ought to apologize directly to the employee. If the employee cannot answer the question, it is clear the manager has not fulfilled their personal responsibility to train the employee. Even if another employee on your team was responsible for training this employee, the leader should still apologize since it remains the leader's responsibility. As we will find out later, a leader can delegate a task, but cannot delegate away the responsibility. If the employee answers the question, "What happened" successfully, a leader should pat himself or herself on the back for a job well done of training the employee. Most likely the employee just made a mistake.

The question after what happened is "Why do you suppose this happened?" Part of proper job instruction is not only to train an employee on what has to be done, but why it needs to be done. People need to understand the logic of why something needs to be done, otherwise an important 7-step process will quickly become a 4-step process. Once again, if the employee cannot answer why this mistake happened, the leader should apologize directly to the employee. If the employee knows why it happened, the leader should pat him or herself on the back for a job well done. Most likely the employee just made a mistake. One important point to remember about mistakes is they will occur. Completely eliminating them is probably unrealistic; reducing them is your goal.

Employees have an expectation that if they make a mistake or fall short of meeting a leader's expectations, the leader will not throw them under the bus. Instead the leader should support them and ask the questions, "What happened?", "Why did this happen?" and the third question, "What can we do differently to prevent it from recurring?" Otherwise, employees who witness other employees being blamed for mistakes when they know they have not been trained to meet expectations, will begin to start thinking they work in a "Death-for-mistake" environment. How demotivating.

When asking the questions, "What happened?" and "Why

did this happen?" it is important to understand the employee is doing the criticizing and the leader is the one who is listening. What is the number one complaint employees have of their manager? The answer is: the manager does not listen. I am of the opinion, no leader should ever think about drilling an employee when they make a mistake. First leaders need to determine if they met the employee's and management's expectation to train correctly.

The third question a leader should ask the employee, "What can we do differently to prevent this from recurring?" is to get the employee involved in the solution so we can hold them accountable. In addition, as we noted earlier, employees bring more energy to their own ideas.

I recall a speaking engagement in Florida where an attendee asked, "What happens if the employee can answer the fact finding questions successfully, yet they continue to make the same mistake over and over again?" I responded, "Human beings do not change unless there is a reason, either a consequence or a reward." If employees continue to make the same mistakes, simply add another fact finding question, "Are you unwilling or incapable of applying your knowledge?" Employees unwilling to apply their knowledge are guilty of insubordination: failure to perform a reasonable request. If employees are incapable of applying their knowledge, this position may not be for them.

It takes courage to be a leader. Earlier I said the best way to gain respect from an employee was to simply listen. Another way of gaining respect from employees is to confront marginal and unsatisfactory performances or behaviors. If the employee commits the same mistake on more than one occasion and they can answer what and why it happened, corrective discipline is one way of guiding the employee to make the right choices regarding their performance or behavior.

Sit down with the employee in private. Let them know that based on your fact finding questions when they committed the mistake, you have determined the employee has been trained to perform the task correctly, however it appears the employee is not applying what they have been taught. You would like the employee to put together a written plan on what they are going to do to prevent the mistake from occurring again. This written plan usually encompasses two or three sentences on what the employee will be doing differently. Once the employee has completed their plan, ask the employee to sign their plan. Requesting an employee's signature ensures accountability. The employee leaves this meeting saying, "Wow, I just told the leader what I was going to do differently."

It is imperative a leader clearly states what the consequence will be if employees fail to abide by their plan. Let employees know they must abide by their plan or a formal verbal warning will be the result. Most employees will make the choice to change their performance or behavior once they receive a verbal warning. However, sometimes a verbal warning is not a great enough consequence, and a leader needs to be willing to bring a written warning, suspension or termination into play.

Involve employees by asking the three coaching questions to assess if you have met your obligation to train them to do the task correctly. Once you have determined the employees have been trained and know better, involve the employees in the solution by having the employees document what will be done differently. Let the employees know the consequence if they do not abide by their plan. If any employees choose not to follow their written plan, who gave them a verbal? The employee did!

All motivation is self-motivation. Leaders do not terminate employees. Employees terminate their own employment. If a manager chooses not to coach an employee through mistakes, they will be creating a "Death-for-mistake" environment. Very demotivating!

Chapter 6
Sink or Swim

A common training technique used by many organizations is known as the "Sink or Swim Method," sometimes called "Baptism by Fire." A manager hires an employee. The manager provides the employee little if any training. If the employee happens to sink the manager tells the boss, "The employee just could not cut it!" Did you catch that part about little if any training was provided? Now, if the employee somehow swims, what does the manager tell the boss? "Look what I developed!" It is amazing how often some managers take credit for good things that happen but won't step up and take the blame for the bad things. Even if the manager doesn't play a role in training the employee, the buck still stops with the manager. The manager can delegate the task; however they cannot delegate away the responsibility.

The Four Steps of Job Instruction method of training is the easiest and surest way to train an employee. The first step is really quite simple. Interview the employee, by asking, "Have you ever done this task before?" If they say, "No, I have not done this task before," you are now dealing with an alien—someone who may take everything you say literally. In fact, if you were training them how to properly lift a box, they might literally try to lift the box with their legs because you told them to do so. If the employee answers, "Yes, I have ten years of experience," you have just learned that there is a good chance the employee will go back to old ways of doing the task because old habits die hard.

The second step is to show and tell the employee not only what steps must be done, but also why it is important the steps be done that way. Many people are visual learners, meaning they need to see how a task needs to be done. When training an employee, it is imperative the employee see the task being done from the right angle. In other words, do not train the employee with them standing opposite of you. The employee should be standing in a manager's hip pocket. Think back to learning to tie a shoe. If the person you are training is opposite you, it is difficult to transpose the steps. One more point, don't wait for an employee to ask permission to stand next to you, invite them.

The third step is to ask the employee to show and tell back to you. I also call this the echo technique. You have no way of knowing what the employee actually understands unless you ask them to restate or summarize what you just said. Whenever sending a message, it is the sender's responsibility to make sure the receiver understands what was communicated. It is not the receiver's responsibility to ask questions.

One Thanksgiving, we invited family to the house to celebrate. My wife asked me if I wanted to clean the kitchen. I said, "Sure!" She then ran upstairs to begin cleaning the bathroom. A short time later, my wife came downstairs and asked if I knew what she meant by, "Clean the kitchen?" I said, "I sure do. You want me to put the dishes in the dishwasher, clean the counters, right?" My wife looked at me and said, "No that is not what I meant. I wanted you to do the dishes, clean the counters, clean underneath the toaster, clean the burners, clean the front of the fridge, sweep and wax the floor." Had my wife never clarified what she meant, my excuse would have been, "I didn't know you meant that. Why didn't you just say so?"

I have met my share of managers who were not effective communicators, yet they had no problem writing communication as a developmental opportunity on an employee's performance review. "Responsibility cannot be divided" is another truth overlooked by today's managers. If a manager ever hears employees respond, "I did my share," or "I did my job," or "No one ever told me," or "I did it last time," these responses do not reflect employees with bad attitudes, but possibly a manager practicing management without a license. If the manager had either told or asked the employees how they were going to break up a job, then they would not have this pandemonium.

At a local fast-food restaurant, they have a bell situated at each exit door. If a customer believes they received excellent customer service, the customer is encouraged to ring the bell, at which point, the employees shout out, "Thank you!"

My daughter had her eyes fixated on the bell. She could not wait to ring the bell and hear the employees respond. There was just one small problem. As we exited she rang the bell, but not one employee shouted. I could see the disappointment on my daughter's face.

I asked my wife to take our daughter and son to the car. I then asked the teenager working behind the counter if I could speak to the manager on duty. In a matter of moments the manager introduced himself and asked how he could be of service. I explained the whole situation. I noted how my daughter rang the bell and not one employee responded with a thank you.

How did the manager respond? "I am sorry sir, it is hard to find good people these days!" I then asked if he put anybody in charge of shouting thank you. He confidently replied, "It is everybody's job to shout thank you." I then asked if he ever heard the expression, "Everybody's responsibility is nobody's responsibility?" He just gave me a blank stare. As I thanked him for his time, I added, "By the way, you can't blame your employees, because the buck stops with you."

This is the same manager that will get his team together in a team meeting and begin sermonizing that they all are responsible for shouting thank you. Had the manager clarified specifically that "between 7pm and 8pm, Mary you are the designated shouter," there would be no need to have a team meeting and rip into everybody on the team.

Put yourself in the shoes of the employees when the manager is giving everyone a speech on the lack of team effort. Might you be thinking, "I am always doing it," or "I did it last time," and might you be thinking how great a job you do, yet still get your butt chewed out? Demotivating!

If a quarterback goes back to pass and is sacked, does the quarterback get off the ground and start screaming at everybody on the team. I think not. The quarterback, if trained correctly, should approach the lineman who did not fulfill their blocking assignment and ask, "What happened?" Envision for a moment, a quarterback who gets off the ground after being sacked and rips into the entire team. Everyone gets ripped, the good guys and the bad guys. Now imagine how hard it will be for the good guys to do their job during the next play. A quick way of gaining respect with employees is to recognize people who deserve to be recognized and confront the people who are not doing the job. Chewing everyone out together is a sign of weakness and employees will question the courage and credibility of the manager.

Watch a car race. When the race car comes into the pits, every pit member knows what they are responsible for doing. Cars are jacked up, tires changes, fuel added, windshields replaced, refreshments provided to the driver, all in a matter of seconds. If the pit manager never clarified what was wanted from each pit employee envision the chaos and pandemonium. Wouldn't that be demotivating?

After you have ensured comprehension, the fourth and final step of job instruction is to have the employee follow up with the leader or designated person a short time later to make sure they are performing the task the way you agreed upon back in step three. If the task is done correctly, recognize the employee. If the employee is not doing the task the way they showed or summarized back to you in step three, ask what happened and why to see if they were trained to meet expectations. If the task is not done correctly and the employee knows what happened and why, did they simply just make a mistake or are they unwilling or incapable of doing it the way you wanted it done?

As much sense as it makes to train someone using the four steps of job instruction, it's not how most employees get trained. Here is a more common scenario. I take my prize employee, who happens to be my informal leader, and ask him to train a new employee on my behalf for the next hour. The informal leader sits the new employee down and begins to lecture about what needs to be done. The informal leader starts using fancy words, phrases and acronyms the new employee has never heard before. You see the informal leader has an agenda. He wants to demonstrate to the new employee how bright he is and how dumb the new employee happens to be.

Once the informal leader explains to the new employee what has to be done, he comes back with the infamous question, "Do you have any questions?" The new employee has a ton of questions to ask, but their common sense kicks in. The new employee thinks, "Every time I ask the informal leader a question, I bet they will see me as being stupid or a poor listener or just maybe the informal leader will take my questions as an insult to his training efforts." Consequently, the employee does not ask as many questions as they should, if they ask any at all. The manager's job just became that much more difficult because they can delegate the task of job instruction to the employee, but the buck stops with them.

Managers who use the sink or swim method when training their employees, managers who do not train their employees to do the job, often will then fall back on progressive discipline to resurrect the employee. The manager is not training the employee, yet they attempt to skirt their responsibility by using discipline. The manager is passing the buck. How many parents after watching their one year old fall down while trying to learn how to walk, would shout, "You suck!" What we really do is pick the toddler off the floor and encourage them to try again. Employees not trained to meet expectations become demotivated employees.

Chapter 7
Recognition

"Atta Boy," "Atta Girl," "Good job," "Keep up the good work," "If you don't hear from me, just assume everything went well." These are familiar expressions managers use to recognize the efforts of their employees. I often ask attendees, "Where did you learn to recognize people this way?" They answer they learned from their parents, teachers and past bosses. In their minds, based on their personal value system, these people think they are recognizing employees effectively. They recognize employees by saying things like "good job," and "nice work, people." Some do it every day. Others only do it once in a great while.

They mean well, but if you want recognition to stick it has to be sincere, specific and timely. The above attempts at recognition lack specifics and consequently don't always sound sincere. "Thanks for staying 10 minutes late yesterday, we met our deadline because of your efforts" or "Thanks for providing me the data for my report, it made my job easier" are examples of genuine recognition.

Recognition is a basic human need. Nature's law of distribution says that some employees will need to be recognized more often than others. We have nicknames for those that have a high need to be recognized: suck-up, needy, high maintenance, brown-noser, and glory hound to name a few. People with a high need of recognition are not bad people. They just have a different value system from their co-workers.

Most people gained a need to be recognized in school. Kindergarten teachers did a wonderful job of letting us know how we were doing by using happy and sad faces. In grade school it was letter grades. Even through college, professors had the nerve to let us know how we were doing. When we got to the real world and started working for a living, we still wanted to hear how we were doing. In fact, the number one question on the mind of every employee is, "How am I doing?"

If employees must wait until their performance review to find out how they are doing, then sadly the manager is not doing the job. Most likely, if the employee finds out they have a couple areas of improvement for the first time during the performance review, they will naturally get defensive and suddenly develop a bad attitude. Once again, the manager is responsible for the employee becoming demotivated. This is the same manager who complains about how the employees don't accept criticism well during a performance review. Insanity!

I asked a student during a class discussion, why they liked performance reviews. The student said, "I get to find out how I am doing and I get recognized." I followed up, "That's too bad you have to wait until the annual performance to find out how you are doing and to be recognized." An HR executive told me many years ago, a performance review ought to be nothing more and nothing less than a summary of everything a leader has discussed with the employee since the most recent performance review.

Recognition can be very motivational with employees. They typically will make a choice to work faster, harder and smarter when the leader pays them a sincere compliment. In most cases, recognition does not cost any money and falls under a leader's control.

There are a few managers who do not like to be recognized themselves. They sometimes make a choice to not recognize their employees because they think it is already in their employees' paychecks. This is an example of managers imposing their value systems on their employees.

An interesting thing about recognition is the type of reaction you will get. Most employees appreciate and need recognition, and will choose to work smarter, faster and harder to get it. A few, however, may react defensively or even a bit suspiciously. Employees reflecting these behaviors often had previous managers who attempted to use recognition as a means of manipulating them to do something. We all have heard of the carrot and stick mentality! A manager recognizes an employee for working overtime, and then subsequently asks the employee to work overtime again. If a manager is going to use recognition as a manipulation tool, employees will avoid the manager like the plague, and learn to flinch if someone says "good job!" A manager using recognition as a manipulative tool possibly had teachers and parents who were guilty at one time or another of doing so.

One manager claimed he did not get a reaction at all from the employee. I asked the manager if he would be more likely or less likely to recognize that person again. He admitted less likely. I then asked the manager my all-time favorite question: "Do you have an open mind?" Predictably the manager said yes. I explained that every action has a reaction. I went on to explain that there was a reaction, but he was just not the one to see it. The reaction could be underneath or the reaction could have come out when they got home and told their significant other that the manager recognized them. The employee simply didn't give the manager the satisfaction of knowing it made her feel good. If a manager starts feeling sorry for herself because she didn't get a positive reaction, that would be a symptom of a manager who is using recognition for self-gratification. This manager is recognizing the employee because the manager wants to feel better. That would be the wrong reason to recognize an employee.

Group recognition is a common way managers go about paying a compliment. Typically, the manager recognizes an employee in front of the rest of the group. If the employee has thick skin, then they can easily put up with all the flack they will get from others after the fact. If the employee has thin skin, while they are being recognized in front of the group, under their breath they probably are saying, "Shut up manager, I have to work with these people." When it comes to group recognition the rule is: get an employee's permission to recognize them in front of their peers. If they say they do not want to be recognized, respect their choice and move on. A manager should never recognize an employee because the manager wants to feel good.

Occasionally, I get called on by Human Resources to resolve conflicts between an employee and a manager. I recall sitting down with one employee and trying to determine how I could help improve the relationship between him and his manager. The employee just sat there staring at the floor. I then asked the employee, "What does your manager do to tick you off everyday?" The employee's eyes just lit up. He indicated that the manager just gave him a verbal warning for not coming to work everyday on time. I asked him if it was justified. He nodded in agreement. However, what really ticked him off was that he made an effort to come to work everyday for five straight days and the manager never once noticed. He added that the manager always found time to notice everybody else on the team. I thanked the employee for providing me feedback.

A short time later I sat down with this employee's manager and asked if this problem employee ever did anything worthy of recognition? He looked at me and said, "The employee doesn't do jack squat! Why should I recognize him?" I informed the manager the employee made an effort to come to work every day on time for the last 5 days and he has yet to be recognized. I asked the manager if this employee was making his job easier or harder by making a choice to come to work on time. The manager muttered, "Easier." The moral of this story is everyone needs to be recognized regardless of where they might be on the bell curve.

For years the popular way to recognize an employee was a pat on the back. However, a minority of people wrecked it for everyone; it came down to the location of that pat on the back. Don't do it unless you want to be sued one of these days. Today, the number one way to recognize an employee is in handwriting. When a leader puts a message that is sincere, specific and timely on a sticky note or piece of paper, it typically is received a bit differently. Most employees will read the handwritten recognition and then file it away. Some rainy day that employee will start to clean out a file and read the note again. Handwritten recognition is better than all other forms of recognition because it is tangible. It reminds the employee how they made a difference.

Not all employees file away handwritten recognition. Extroverts will slap that sticky note on their chest or somewhere near their workstation so everybody can see they made a difference. Introverts would never post the note in public. That goes against their value system. Instead they take the note and put it inside a file drawer or in their tool box, so they can be the only people to see it.

Recognition is a basic human need. Some employees need to hear it more than others. Get to know your employees. If you really want to get creative, use a Circle Six with your team and ask, "What are some ways I can better recognize you?" You likely will be stunned by the amount of ideas you collect that do not cost any money and fall under your control. As you act on your employee's ideas you gain respect. Don't forget to follow up with employees on their ideas even if you are not going to use them. This encourages them to participate in the Circle Six process in the future.

Chapter 8
Delegate Authority

I like to ask seminar attendees, "What is the first thing that comes to your mind when I say, 'authority'?" Most responses center on the ability to tell people what to do. In fact, one attendee responded, "For years people were telling me what to do! Now that I got promoted, I can't wait to start telling others what to do!" Sadly, that response reflects a common misconception regarding authority. Telling others what to do or throwing one's weight around is not authority. Authority is defined as a person's ability to act or decide.

Most people's perception of authority comes from how their parents or managers exercised their authority. Today, the number one reason why an employee leaves an organization happens to be the manager. A manager not trusting an employee to act and decide for a majority of the day will lead to a demotivated employee and send the employee job shopping.

A majority of Generation Y, Generation X and Baby Boomer employees like to work for leaders who trust their decision making ability. If not trusted, employees do not feel appreciated, which eventually will lead to demotivated employees or, even worse, good employees that decide to work for your competitor.

The whole world spins on authority: who has it; who wants it; and who doesn't do anything with their authority. When a manager delegates a task, they also are delegating the decision making authority that goes along with that task. It is implied or inherent that decision making is part of completing the task. Leaders have an obligation to train employees to make decisions that go along with the tasks they are paid to do. Not doing so indicates the manager is a micro-manager or dictator. Organizations look for participative leaders, those leaders willing to trust the decision making ability of their employees. Under participative leaders, employees will bring energy, creativity, and passion to their position.

For years, a dictatorial management style was the preferred style mainly due to the values generated by the military. From 1900 through the 1970s, the military exercised the draft to fill the military ranks. When they got out of the military, and sought out a job or profession, guess what management style these ex-military brought to work? They used what they had learned, a militant dictator style.

The draft was discontinued after the Vietnam War, and participative management began to take hold. Today, the Red Cross, the U.S. Military and CIA routinely are the only professions looking for a dictatorial management style.

Acting independently is the highest level of authority, but if an employee makes a decision or acts on his own and doesn't tell anyone including his manager, this can easily lead to a frustrated manager or co-workers. This is one of the most abused levels of authority, either because it's overused or underused. Some employees hang out on this level too often and some do not hang out on this level at all. When employees choose not to communicate their decision to co-workers, it may prove to be very frustrating because co-workers feel they need to be in the loop. Nobody in an organization acts independently all the time. Even the CEOs have to inform board members or other executives of decisions they make.

Acting or deciding, then informing others after the fact is another level of authority. Timing is the critical issue here. If an employee waits to tell a manager of a decision they made three weeks earlier, they actually have been acting independently. If an employee has been empowered to spend up to $300 in the best interest of the organization, the last place they should be is in their manager's office asking permission. This employee has been empowered to act. Their only decision should be if they are going to inform others after the fact or act independently.

Asking permission, then acting is an often misunderstood level. Employees given the authority to act on their own, who still ask permission to make a decision, waste their time and that of the manager. Anyone (manager or employee) in a position for greater than 12-18 months should be making most decisions on their own.

Over the years I have asked managers why they chose not to delegate authority as often as they should. Barring a few exceptions, most of the reasons fall under either not trusting the employee or facing resistance from the employee. Let's take a look at each of these responses in greater detail.

If delegated to properly, most employees will be happy you are empowering them to get things done. Generation Y, Generation Xers, and Baby Boomers all possess a need to be trusted. I suspect none of these generations drive to work each day saying, "I can't wait for the manager not to trust me today!" In fact, being empowered can be very motivating for an employee. Since empowering employees improves productivity, let's take a look at how to delegate authority.

The next time an employee asks permission to do something, and you know they really should be making this decision on their own, simply ask the employee, "Why are you asking me permission?" Most likely their response will center on, "It has always been this way" or "You are the manager." If that is the case, a manager should apologize directly to the employee for never making it perfectly clear they had the power to act. Why apologize? One of the fundamentals of responsibility is "Responsibility must be given with sufficient authority." In other words, when delegating a task, a manager has an obligation to communicate the authority going along with that task.

When delegating authority, if the employee is reluctant or apprehensive, a leader can ask, "Why the reluctance?" Most of my supervision students initially think an employee is reluctant in assuming authority because they are afraid they will make a mistake. I beg to differ. Employees do not fear mistakes; employees fear the consequences that go along with the mistake.

If any employee is concerned about the consequences, a leader better communicate what the consequences will be. Let the employee know what to expect. I would communicate to the employee, "If you make a mistake, first of all I am going to support you and not throw you under the bus." Secondly, I would let the employee know if they make a mistake, I am going to ask them a few questions, like "What happened?", "Why did this happen?", and "What are we going to do differently?" A leader needs to ask these questions to determine if the leader met their obligation to train the employee. If an employee cannot tell you what happened or why it happened, remember the buck stops with the leader! A leader can delegate a task or decision making, but they cannot delegate away their own responsibility.

The most popular of all fundamentals of responsibility is "Responsibility for final results cannot be delegated away." A leader can delegate a task, project or decision making to any of their employees, however, if the work is not done correctly or on time, the buck stops with them. The leader cannot blame the employee to higher-ups. The leader must step up to the plate and accept the blame if work is not done correctly in the leader's area.

When delegating authority, a leader may run into the response, "That's your job, don't pawn your job off on me!" If the employee is resistant to making decisions, kindly remind the employee that resisting the delegation is a form of insubordination. Delegating authority is not negotiable. It is inherent or implied whenever a leader delegates a task. Along with the responsibility the leader is also delegating the authority needed to get the job done.

This past year my wife and I put our house up for sale. If you've ever attempted to sell a home, you are well aware of the inopportune times a phone call comes from a realtor indicating a buyer wants to walk through your home. I can recall one Saturday morning, when we got a call to get out by 9am. That gave us approximately half an hour to get the house into prime shape. My wife instructed our kids to go upstairs and clean. She asked if I could clean the kitchen. My wife said she was going to straighten up the living room. About two minutes later,

I heard some shouting taking place between our two kids. I heard Gina saying, "Mom, Matt is in my room, he is telling me what to do!" I then heard Gina say, "Matt, you are not the boss of me!"

Just then, my wife asked what all the shouting upstairs was about. I said, "Dear, you never clarified what you wanted them to do, in addition, you never clarified if one of the kids had authority over the other." My wife looked at me and said, "Dear, if you have all the answers, would you please smooth things over upstairs." The moral of the story is: if you ever hear an employee say, "Who died and made you boss?" that expression is not a symptom of an employee with a bad attitude. It is a symptom of a manager practicing management without a license.

The final truth is that responsibility must be given with sufficient authority. If a manager delegates any authority to an employee, be it temporary or permanent, they have an obligation to communicate to all other workers who might be impacted by this employee's decision making ability. If a manager chooses not to communicate authority, I suspect there will be a meeting taking place in the future to correct what should never have happened to begin with. When managers choose not to communicate authority, it can be very demotivating to their employees.

There are some managers who try to justify their own job security by making decisions their employees should be making. These are the same managers who will complain how busy they are running around putting out fires, and how their employees sit around and wait to be told and have bad attitudes.

Managers often mistake acting macho for being a decision

maker. For example, if you walk into your boss's office and say with authority, "I am going to ask Michelle to work overtime so we can meet that deadline," don't kid yourself; this isn't acting or deciding. You're leaving it up to the boss, because the boss can say "No you are not!" The only time a manager or employee is acting and informing is when the action is already done. For example, "Michelle worked overtime yesterday; we met the deadline!"

There are certain risks if an employee spends most of their day asking permission even though they have been empowered. The first risk is they will get the reputation of someone who cannot make a decision. Good luck on getting promoted.

The second risk an employee runs is the risk of the manager saying "No" to their best ideas. We can all think of at least one time in our professional careers where we walked into our manager's office with what we thought was a great idea but they didn't. As we left their office feeling sorry for ourselves, we thought, "Why didn't I just act and inform the manager after the fact?"

The final risk of asking permission is the employee will not grow and develop. Any employee will find it difficult to grow if someone else is making decisions for them. The irony is managers are supposed to play a role in the growth and development of their employees. A manager who doesn't play a role in positioning their employee to be promoted is grooming a demotivated employee.

It is perfectly fine to ask permission if an employee is new to a particular position. It is only reasonable that an employee should be asking permission during the training phase of their position. Asking permission outside of training will not benefit the manager or employee.

I can't underscore the importance of a leader training an employee to meet job expectations enough. One day I sat in my boss's office, complaining about an employee named David. After about 15 seconds, my boss looked at me and said, "Are you complaining Mr. Graci?" Back then I thought I was pretty smooth, and I said, "No, I am just venting." My boss grinned and said, "Mr. Graci, it sounds to me like you are complaining and I do not have time for this, so I will make your life a bit easier." He asked me if I was empowered to train David as I see fit. I said, "Yes." He then asked, "Are you empowered to communicate expectations to David as you see fit?" Again I said, "Yes." Finally, he asked, "Are you empowered to deliver a verbal and written warning to David if he is not meeting your expectations?" One last time I said, "Yes." My manager leaned back in his chair and said, "Great, now get the heck out of my office so I can do my job." As I walked out of his office feeling sorry for myself, my boss threw in one more comment. He said, "John, they do not pay me enough to do your job and mine."

On that day, my boss created a significant emotional event for me. It dawned on me that I had better start acting without my boss's help or I would be out of a job. What concerned me the most is my boss managed via a "Death-for-mistake" type of environment. Meaning, he was okay with his managers making decisions, however they had better not make a mistake. I worked under that that scenario for nine months. Security is a basic human need, and I certainly did not feel secure. How demotivating when managers do not train employees to meet expectations.

Chapter 9
Growth and Development

Baby Boomers, Generation-Xers and Generation-Yers all possess the value of wanting to grow and develop. These generations realize Uncle Sam may not be there for them when they choose to retire. They are taking personal responsibility for themselves by making it a point to be continually open to taking on new skills and challenges in order to put them into a better position to be promoted. One way to help an employee meet their need to grow and develop is to delegate tasks and authority.

There are some employees who just do not have a high need to grow and develop. I would still delegate to these employees. Everyone gets delegated to! If managers choose to delegate tasks just to employees who are cooperative and willing, they will soon be grooming demotivated employees. Eventually, these cooperative and willing employees will look around and ask themselves why they're the only people being delegated to? Underneath, they will start to question the credibility of the manager, because the manager seems unwilling or unable to delegate to everyone.

The reasons a manager chooses not to delegate can be unlimited. Most of the barriers preventing a manager from delegating are just plain excuses. A common reason a manager chooses not to delegate to an employee is a lack of trust. Well, who hired the employee? The manager may have to take responsibility for hiring an employee they cannot trust. Train to trust. That's where the four steps of job instruction come into play. If managers surround themselves with employees they cannot trust, the managers wind up doing their employees' jobs in addition to their own. Ironically, these are the same managers who will complain about their employees. Sounds like insanity to me!

Some managers choose not to delegate as often as they should because they are trying to justify their own job and create job security by doing the work of their employees. The biggest downside here is that upper management may ask the question, "Why are we paying this manager a manager's salary when they are doing the work of the employees? They were just in my office complaining how busy they were today, I can see why!" Now how secure is the manager?

Some managers choose not to delegate because they want the credit and recognition that goes along with doing the task. I know somebody else who wants the credit and recognition—the employee! So how can the manager and an employee get the recognition? A manager should delegate a task to an employee. Once the employee completes the task, the manager should recognize the employee. The manager can communicate to their boss how they got the task completed through the employee. That's the kind of recognition I would want. Getting work and decisions completed through my staff makes my hiring decisions, my training techniques, and my leadership skills all look good.

Yes, there are some menial tasks that a manager might delegate to an employee and the employee might not find the task either enjoyable or challenging. So what? How many times do you get to pick and choose what tasks you want delegated to you? Remember the employee has a need to grow and develop. The best way the manager can meet that need is to delegate.

Some managers choose not to delegate to an employee because it makes the manager feel insecure. This employee has little choice but to sit around and complain. Essentially, the manager has groomed a demotivated employee.

During a keynote presentation I delivered in New York, I talked about the importance of helping employees grow and develop and about the importance of a leader effectively delegating to everyone. I then asked the audience for reasons why a manager should not delegate to an employee. An attendee in the front instantly put their arm up. They stated that when it comes to delegation, they do not delegate for two reasons. They fear the employee's responses, "It is not in my paycheck" and "It is not in my job description." I asked the attendee if they had an open mind. They reluctantly said, "Yes." I indicated those phrases are the oldest phrases known to mankind. The reason employees throw out these weak excuses is because they have worked in the past with other managers. I then asked the attendee if they were familiar with the phrase, "other duties as assigned?" He looked at me and smiled a bit. I explained the phrase, "Other duties as assigned" means you can delegate whatever tasks you deem necessary. I then asked the attendee if they get a bump in salary every time their manager delegates to them, and of course he said, "No." I followed up, "Why should an employee get a bump in salary? If all other duties as assigned is in their job description, then it is already in their paycheck."

Employees have an expectation the leader is going to play a role in helping them grow and develop. Upper management holds that same expectation. They believe leaders should be positioning their employees for other jobs within the organization. The only way to meet both the expectation of the employee and management is to delegate! If they don't grow and develop and challenge the employees, these managers will be creating a negative place to work for the employees. Growth and development is a basic human need. If the employee's need to grow and develop is strong enough, they will become demotivated and eventually make the ultimate choice, leaving the organization because we didn't challenge them.

Chapter 10
Dignity and Respect

Who is responsible for providing a new employee with an orientation, Human Resources or the manager? If you answered Human Resources, you've got plenty to learn.

Orientation is about two things, dignity and respect. Essentially, we are taking an employee off the street and communicating to them that we respect them as an employee and we are going to demonstrate our respect by helping them feel dignified. If you doubt that a manager is supposed to play a primary role in orientation, simply sit down with your staff and ask them, "What would you like to have known on the first, second and third day of work?" If you want to listen to everybody, use the Circle Six technique.

Much of what employees are looking for falls under the power and control of the manager. We have all heard of stories where an employee came to work at 8 a.m. with a positive attitude and by 10 a.m. they were gone! Most likely, the employee did not feel valued, may even have felt like a number, so they left in search of another company who would roll out the red carpet for them.

Human Resources does play a role in orientation, but their role pales in comparison to what employees expect from you, their immediate manager. The most common information employees are looking for on the first few days includes:

- introductions;
- work hours;
- where do I get supplies to do my job;
- time cards;
- payroll periods;
- dress code;
- internet policy;
- tardy expectations;
- absenteeism expectations;
- safety expectations;
- cell phone policy;
- tour of facility;
- location of restrooms;
- break times;
- call in sick procedures;
- vacation policy;
- how long they are going to be in training;
- and who to ask questions of when the manager is not around.

Leaders have an obligation to communicate performance expectations to their employees. Performance expectations include quantity, quality and timeliness. For example, instead of just putting employees into training, leaders should let the employees know how long they will be in training, and how long they have to get up to speed to meet the specified expectations.

If a manager does not clearly communicate expectations, an employee will begin to start guessing.

When a leader establishes goals for an employee, the SMART technique can be very helpful. In other words:

- a leader needs to get SPECIFIC on what they want from the employee;
- a leader needs to make that goal MEASURABLE;
- a leader needs to make the goal ALIGNED with corporate objectives;
- a leader needs to make the goal REALISTIC;
- and finally a leader needs to attach a TIMELINE to the goal and follow up accordingly to ensure they are doing everything they can to help the employee.

A leader has an obligation to communicate behavioral expectations too. I like to call these behavioral expectations a manager's "hot buttons." Attendance, tardiness, safety, dress code, language, cell phone usage, horseplay, internet usage are just a few "hot buttons" that need to be discussed with an employee.

A common response from the team of a manager who doesn't clearly communicate behavioral expectations, would be, "I didn't know you meant that. If it was so important to you, why didn't you just say something?" Once again, the response reflects a manager practicing management without a license.

Think of behavioral expectations as preventive discipline. If the importance of behaving a certain way is clearly communicated from the leader to the employee, it will become important to the employee. In fact, there is so much information to be communicated a checklist is helpful so you don't forget.

One class I conducted for a manufacturer in Duluth, Minnesota created a checklist of over fifty items participants wanted to know on the first day. Then we started to break the list down between what items fell under a manager's control versus Human Resources. After getting through just half of the orientation items, the class started to make fun of how deficient they thought their orientation process was at their company.

I asked for two volunteers to help me remove a banner located on the back wall of the training room. The banner read, "XYZ Company, The Employer of Choice in Duluth, MN." The class sat in disbelief as I acted out trying to take down the banner. I then looked at the class and said, "Your organization wants to be the employer of choice in Duluth. I have just learned your organization is not even covering many of the items on the checklist and you think it is funny."

I continued, "Let me get this right, you have employees who start up on the first day with ambition and motivation. Trust me when I say, they are not feeling respected. They complain about the poor first day they had because they did not feel respected or dignified." I continued, "Save the speech about wanting to be the employer of choice. It is not working. If you personally want to be respected as a manager, go out and earn it by treating employees the way you would want to be treated. If you choose not to help employees feel dignified, you have groomed a demotivated employee."

After class, the Operations Manager approached me and asked if I thought I might have been too hard on the employees. I asked the Operations Manager if he had an open mind, and predictably, he said, "yes." I told him, "It's your fault your orientation process is a mess. The buck stops with you! I suggest you hold your managers accountable for what they are

learning here today and watch as your job becomes easier."
The Operations Manager simply replied, "You certainly don't
mince words."

If leaders want to be respected, they better demonstrate respect
to employees. Managers who feel entitled to respect based on
their position are only kidding themselves. Treat employees
the way you want to be treated and they will give you respect.
Treat an employee like a number, and you have groomed a
demotivated employee. Even if Human Resources plays a larger
role with orientation than average, a manager needs the respect
more than Human Resources. Go out and earn it by treating
employees the way you want to be treated.

Chapter 11
Do Employees Resist Change?

At one time the world's knowledge doubled every 200 years. Today, due to technology, the world's knowledge doubles every two to three years. Ideas are being generated at a record pace. What does this mean to today's leaders? Things are changing at a faster pace than ever before and managers had better be pretty good at communicating change to their employees.

Organizations need to change. That's how they stay competitive, improve and even survive. Upper management expects leaders on every level to be proficient at getting employees to accept a change of methods, procedures, policies, conditions, and more.

Grocery stores reflect just how rampant change can be. It wasn't long ago that a shopper would need to travel to several different stores to get the week's errands completed. Today, grocery stores offer many more services and products than they did just a few years ago. Flowers, liquor, dry cleaning, banking, photography, hair salons, restaurants, and a host of other offerings can now be found inside grocery stores. Can you even imagine a grocery chain unwilling to sell these products or services? They would lose customers!

I have asked audiences across the country the question, "Do employees resist change?" I repeatedly hear "Yes!" shouted with despair and confidence. Employees don't resist change nearly as much as they object to the manner in which it is communicated to them. "When is management going to understand this is the real world down here?" and "It will never work here!" are common responses to proposed changes. Both reflect resistance and a demotivated employee.

Today's leaders need to be more proactive than ever. They need to anticipate how their employees will respond. Change is relative. In other words, change impacts people differently.

A summer day that's sunny and 75 degrees may be greeted with open arms by golfers and joggers. Farmers praying for moisture or an employee just returning from a rain-soaked vacation might see things differently.

A manager may think a change of procedure is going to make the employee's job easier while making customers happier. The employee may see the change as making their job more difficult. Some employees have a value system that puts them at ease with changes, they like being on the cutting edge of change. They see most changes as the best thing since sliced bread. You will also have employees who possess value systems that resist any change from the start.

There are two types of changes a leader has an obligation to attempt to get their employees to accept: mandated changes (those that come from someone other than the leader and thus the leader doesn't control) and those that come from the leader and do fall under the leader's control.

Mandated changes can be the more difficult of the two types. With mandated changes, most likely upper management has come up with a new procedure or policy during a meeting in which some members of line management might not have been in attendance. Upper management now asks the line managers to get their employees to accept the change and put it into place. In short, the line managers did not play a role in developing the mandated changes, but they have been asked to communicate these changes to their team nonetheless. Communicating a layoff or downsizing effort of the organization is an example of mandated change.

Communicating changes that fall under a leader's control is the second type of change. Since the change falls within a leader's decision making authority, the leader has the option to get the employees involved from the start. Cross training is an example of a change that falls under a leader's authority.

Regardless of which type of change a leader is communicating, the objective is to get the staff to accept the change. There are a few rules of thumb when it comes to communicating mandated changes in order to heighten employee acceptance.

A leader needs to focus on communicating the facts behind the change as well as communicating who is benefiting from the change. In addition, since most mandates do not come with a plan of implementation, a leader can involve their employees in how they will apply this change to their area.

Using the example of a company layoff, a leader could communicate the facts supporting the layoff, and then ask employees to voice the benefits of this decision. Do this using the Circle Six technique and the leader can add in benefits if the employees have a hard time seeing them. Facts help employees understand how management arrives at the changes. It might even be helpful if management discussed other possible solutions considered prior to making the decision, how management arrived at the decision, how each department might consider applying the change to their area, and exactly who is benefiting directly and indirectly from the change.

There are some changes that are easy for an employee to accept, however the more complex the change, the more obligation the leader has to help employees accept the change. Since employees do not resist change nearly as much as the manner in which it is communicated, I suspect most employees will appreciate the leader's efforts to help them understand and accept the change.

Changes that fall under a leader's control are the easiest to communicate. Here are few things a leader can do to get employees involved early on in the process. A leader can ask employees:

- To gather facts regarding the situation;
- To help generate solutions;
- To help choose the solutions;
- For ideas on implementing the solution;
- For the benefits of making this change.

Every day leaders are asked to get employees to embrace new methods, new equipment, new materials, and more. Even with a leader's best efforts to communicate a change, an employee may still resist the change. When employees come to work each day, they harbor a built-in bias on how they look at changes—they see changes from their own perspective. Every time a leader communicates to employees, the employees internalize the leader's decisions and changes as to how it will affect them personally.

Leaders have an obligation to help employees understand why management wants them to change. Employees do not resist change nearly as much as they resist that manner in which it is communicated.

Chapter 12
What Unions Know

For years unions focused on manufacturing environments, however, since the year 2000 unions have changed their focus. They still have one eye on manufacturing, but are also closely monitoring call centers, the nursing profession, and clerical/ administrative positions. Unions have heard that managers from these professions are not using their common sense in dealing with their employees, that managers aren't meeting employees' needs. Unions are in the people needs fulfilling business and are keenly aware of the conditions employees desire at work.

Take for instance an employee's need to be listened to. Unions are very good at encouraging shop stewards to walk around daily and ask employees how things are going, how is the manager treating them, how are the conditions, etc. If shop stewards don't like what they hear, they file a grievance against the manager. Unions typically encourage employees to bring their problems first to the shop steward and then to the manager.

Employees have a need to feel secure at work, and unions know exactly how to fulfill that need. Unions are very adept at holding managers accountable for communicating expectations, coaching and training employees to meet expectations. Terminating an employee can be more challenging in a union environment. The benefits unions offer and the seniority system utilized all contribute to helping their members feel secure.

Unions are also known for helping employees feel as though they are part of a team. Associated might even be a better word to describe this need. Union dues are required to join. Meetings are conducted at union halls. Unions provide bumper sticks, hats, and jackets promoting brotherhood and sisterhood. Unions even have company picnics, excluding non-union employees.

Sometimes I get phone calls from past clients in a panic over the belief their employees might be considering joining a union. The client typically wants my expertise on what they can do to prevent their employees from making a choice to join the union. After fact finding to better understand their situation, I usually discover employees are considering joining a union because managers are not applying the fundamentals of leadership. The stunned looks of disbelief are quickly followed by "What can you do Mr. Graci?" I respond that it is not what I can do, but what their upper management team needs to do. I suggest the senior levels of the organization need to start holding managers accountable for what they learned in my classes.

Other times I hear managers from office environments say they are not the least bit worried about a union ever coming on-site. My comeback: "Might an employee choose to leave an organization if a manager chooses not to fulfill their most basic needs?" Don't forget the buck stops with you!

The bottom line is managers who currently work in manufacturing, call centers, nursing and clerical/administrative professions need to understand unions have essentially placed a bulls-eye on their backs. As one union representative proudly exclaimed to me at the end of a keynote presentation, "If managers choose not to fulfill the most basic needs employees have when they come to work, the company may as well put a big green neon sign outside on the front of the building that says, "Union! Come on in!" Now that is common sense!

Chapter 13
An Immense Amount of Power

One of the more challenging areas of my profession is telling clients what they need to hear, not what they want to hear. I am asked to address issues involving employees' productivity or demotivated employees. Often clients ask, "What's next? We really liked what you taught during Supervision I. What is next to help alleviate the problems?" My answer stuns them.

There is an old expression, "Common Sense Isn't Common." The expression illustrates that common sense behavior exhibited by one person, certainly is not the same common sense behavior you see with other people. The techniques and skills required by a leader to create a positive place to work can be regarded as just plain common sense; however, some managers make choices not to apply their common sense.

What is next is not Supervision II. What's next rests in getting managers to apply what they learned during Supervision I. We need to hold people accountable for using the skills they learn. Today's leaders need to fully understand they possess an immense amount of power and authority. Leaders have the power to apply their knowledge when it comes to creating a positive place to work, but they also have the same power not to apply their knowledge. Since leaders are judged on their employees' performance and behavior, why wouldn't leaders want to apply their knowledge of these skills and techniques that easily fall under their control and cost no money to perform?

If today, you don't apply the knowledge you gained from this book, who made that choice? You did of course! Yes, all motivation is self-motivation. By the way, if you choose not to apply your knowledge, you can't go back to a local bar or workout facility and complain about your employees' poor attitudes. That would an example of insanity—doing the same thing over and over and being stunned when nothing ever changes.

But, if you choose to:

- Listen to everybody
- Recognize the efforts people make
- Train them properly
- Coach them through mistakes
- Involve them in change
- Refuse to practice favoritism
- Accept different value systems
- Let them know where they stand
- Challenge them to grow and develop
- And treat them with respect

You will create a motivational work environment in which most employees will respond with a good attitude, and make choices that make your job easier. It's just common sense.

Looking for a speaker?

Author and leadership motivational speaker John Graci sends the message loud and clear: *Leaders have the power to help employees feel good when they come to work, but they also have that same power to make employees feel miserable.*

John's nationally recognized keynote presentation, *"Motivating Employees Using Common Sense,"* provides practical methods to help your leaders improve productivity and morale of their employees. *NEWS FLASH: These common sense methods don't cost any money and fall under a leader's control!*

As seen on CNN, John's sense of humor, charisma and passion blend nicely with his pragmatic style. Meeting planners rave about the benefits.

When you combine the charisma, passion and energy Graci brings to a room, with a wonderful sense of humor spawned from his days as a major market radio announcer, you have the necessary ingredients for an entertaining speaker.

John has delighted audiences from Fortune 500 companies to small business owners for the past 10 years with his practical approach to motivation. He's performed at locations from the Mirage in Las Vegas to overnight company retreats in International Falls, Minnesota!

John's ability to rapidly produce "Ah Ha" moments will instantly create an environment where your leaders will be open to change, thus more receptive to taking on the skills they need to be effective in their position.

For information on classes and speakers
Or to inquire about John Graci's availability
Please contact John Graci
Main: 763-253-9100
Direct: 763-253-9117
Toll Free: 888-242-1359
Fax: 763-253-9191
Email: JohnG@EmployersInc.com
Or visit our web site at www.EmployersInc.com
Search: Graci

Testimonials
from
"Motivating Employees Using Common Sense"

"John is 100% accurate. It is stunning how often leaders choose not to apply their common sense when supervising employees – yet they have the nerve to go to a local bar and complain about bad attitudes of their employees."
-Bill, V.P. Manufacturing New York, NY

"John's presentation is from an in-the-trenches perspective as opposed to out-of-a-textbook."
-Lisa, Call Center Manager Orlando, FL

"I had close to 15 years of management experience, thus I was skeptical about attending. I quickly learned I had 15 years of experience doing things the hard way!"
-Tom, Health Care Administrator Las Vegas, NV

"John possesses a firm grasp of the obvious. Coupled with his tell-it-like-it-is speaking style, I quickly realized the unintended consequences of my actions."
-Catherine, Director of Information and Technology Dallas, TX

Employers Association, Inc
9805 45th Avenue North
Plymouth, MN 55442

Delivering the most popular leadership classes
in the Midwest
and throughout the U.S.
for over 30 years

- Supervision I: Fundamentals of Leadership
- Supervision II: The Next Stage for Improving
  Performance
- Project Management
- Leadership for Leads

About the Author

John Graci has over 15 years of experience in leadership development and training. He is a speaker and consultant for Employers Association, Inc., a leading provider of human resources consulting. His audiences have ranged from Fortune 500 companies to small business owners and include ConAgra, Best Buy, and Andersen Corporation.

LaVergne, TN USA
05 January 2010
168863LV00002B/1/P